Date Due

BC 3 78		
Hensall		
MAY 2 4		
OCT 2 4		
DEC 1 8 1984		
OCT 2 8 1986		
JAN 2 9 1987		
APR 4 1987		
MAR 2 1 1989		

11708

```
j971.3   Harrington, Lyn.
 Har       Ontario.  Chicago, Childrens Press,
         1975.
           96 p.  illus., maps.  (Enchantment of
         Canada)



           1. Ontario.
         0516040715                    0106151 LC
```

6/HE/eN

Enchantment of Canada
Ontario

by Lyn Harrington

 CHILDRENS PRESS, CHICAGO

Acknowledgments

Photograph on page 58 courtesy of Martin Oudejans, Photographer; photographs on pages 32, 34, and 35 courtesy of Ontario Ministry of Natural Resources; photographs on page 51 courtesy of Ontario Ministry of Colleges and Universities. All other photographs courtesy of the Ontario Ministry of Industry and Tourism. Photographs assembled by Robert Trotter, Head, Department of Journalism, Conestoga College of Applied Arts and Technology, Doon, Ontario.

Joan Downing: Editor/Designer
Typesetting by Graphic Services Corporation, Chicago, Illinois
Donald G. Bouma: Map Artist

LIBRARY OF CONGRESS
CATALOGING IN PUBLICATION DATA

Harrington, Lyn
   Ontario.
   (Enchantment of Canada)

   SUMMARY: Introduces the geography, history, resources, industries, way of life, people, and tourist attractions of Ontario, Canada's second largest province.
   1. Ontario—Juvenile literature. [1. Ontario]
I. Title.
F1057.4.H37   971.3'04   74-32340
ISBN 0-516-04071-5

1 2 3 4 5 6 7 8 9 10 11 12 R 78 77 76 75

Contents

A True Tale
To Set the Scene

GOLD IS WHERE YOU FIND IT

In 1901, people in southern Ontario didn't know much about the
northern part of their province. Few of them were excited when a
large area of good farmland was found north of North Bay. The
provincial government decided to build a railway to the Clay Belt.

Many grumbled, "They are wasting our taxes to bring a few potatoes
to market. Northern Ontario is nothing but rocks and bush, a country
for trappers, not farmers."

Yet the railway was begun, and it proved a road to riches. A few
miles south of Haileybury, silver was discovered, mixed with cobalt.

The railway crept farther north. In 1909, a prospector named Harry
Preston found rich seams of gold at Porcupine Lake. That started a
gold rush.

Benny Hollinger, a barber still in his teens, and Alex Gillies, a little
older, had prospected together for two summers. Now they looked for

someone who would supply them with a grubstake for a trip to the Porcupine area. One man put up forty-five dollars for half of what Benny might find. Another gave Alex one hundred dollars for half of his discoveries.

The young prospectors loaded their canoe, food, and drilling equipment onto the train. From the end of the unfinished railway, they canoed west through rocky country covered with spruce trees and moss. They met Harry Preston on the south shore of Porcupine Lake.

Preston told the young men how he had made his discovery. "I just happened to slip on a big rock, and the heel of my boot stripped away the moss, showing a ragged vein of gold. We staked all the land around here. You might find something farther west where Reuben D'Aigle prospected last year."

Benny and Alex took his advice, and paddled into white rock country. They found the pit D'Aigle had dug and the tools he had left. D'Aigle knew about washing gold in Alaskan rivers but nothing about getting it out of hard rock.

The white quartz looked discouraging, but the young men decided to stake a few claims. They cut posts to mark the corners of each claim, then began to strip off the moss to examine the rock.

Suddenly Benny gave a shout and threw his hat in the air. "Gold! Hey, Alex, come and look!"

Alex Gillies rushed over to the white rock. It looked as though someone had dripped a candle along it—but the splashes were shining gold.

The seam stretched for sixty feet, right across the portage trail between two lakes. Trappers and fur traders, geologists and prospectors had walked over it, not knowing of the treasure under their feet.

Benny Hollinger chose the six claims to the west. He soon sold his share to Noah Timmins, who became "the Grand Old Man of Canadian mining."

A mining company took up Alex Gillies' claim. They rushed a crew into the bush to drill the area and bring the samples back to town. The rock drill cores were heavy, and there were hundreds of them. How many could be carried out to the railway before winter came?

The engineer chose cores that showed a trace of gold. He didn't realize that the other cores were much richer. The mining company lost interest, and Timmins bought the claims. That was the beginning of the Hollinger Mine, the greatest gold producer in Canadian history.

"Gold is where you find it," prospectors say.

Reuben D'Aigle and the engineer would add, "But you have to know what you're looking at when you find it!"

Gold is only one of the minerals produced by Ontario.
Shown below are some of the province's other minerals.

The Face of the Land

The Province of Ontario is situated in the middle of Canada and
in the middle of North America. Its southern boundary stretches from
Manitoba through the Great Lakes to Quebec. This border with the
United States, nearly 1,500 miles long, is not guarded by soldiers. It is
proof of the long friendship between Canadians and Americans.

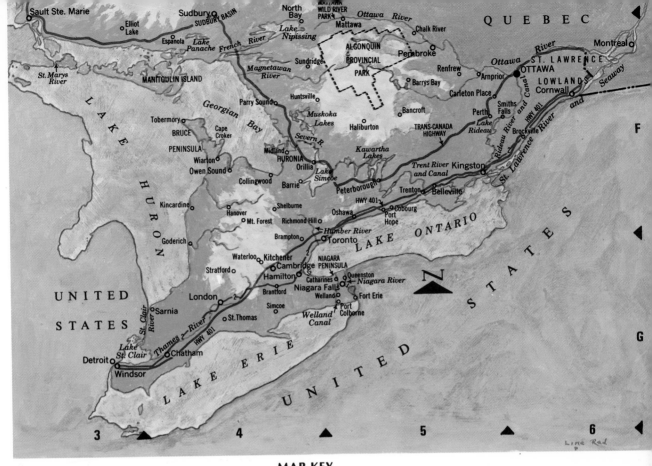

MAP KEY

An asterisk (*) after location indicates enlarged "Triangle" area map above.

Agawa Bay, E-3
Akimiski Island, C-4
Albany River, D-3
Algonquin
   Provincial Park, F-5*
Armstrong, D-2
Arnprior, F-6*
Attawpiskat, C-4
Attawpiskat River, C-3
Bancroft, F-5*
Barrie, F-5*
Barrys Bay, F-5*
Belleville, F-5*
Big Beaver House, C-2
Big Trout Lake, C-2
Brampton, G-5*
Brantford, G-5*
Brockville, F-6*
Bruce Peninsula, F-4*
Cambridge, G-5*
Carleton Place, F-6*
Casummit Lake, C-1
Chalk River, F-5*
Chapleau, E-4
Chatham, G-4*
Cobalt, E-5
Cobourg, G-5*
Cochrane, E-4
Collingwood, F-4*
Collins, D-2
Cornwall, F-6*
Deer Lake, C-1
Dryden, D-1
Elliot Lake, F-4*
Espanola, F-4*
Fort Albany, C-4

Fort Erie, G-5*
Fort Hope, C-2
Fort Severn, B-3
Fort William
   Indian Reserve, E-2
Fraserdale, D-4
French River, F-4*
Georgian Bay, F-4*
Goderich, G-4*
Gogoma, E-4
Great Clay Belt, D-4
Haileybury, E-5
Haliburton, F-5*
Hamilton, G-5*
Hanover, G-4*
Hearst, D-4
Highway 401, F-5*
   F-6*, G-4*
Hudson Bay, A
Hudson Bay Lowlands, C-3
Humber River, G-5*
Huntsville, F-5*
Huronia, F-5*
Jacobs, D-2
James Bay, C-4
Kapuskasing, D-4
Kawartha Lakes, F-5*
Kenora, D-1
Kincardine, F-4*
Kingston, F-6*
Kirkland Lake, E-5
Kitchener, G-4*
Lac Seul, D-1
Lake Abitibi, E-4
Lake Erie, G-4*
Lake Huron, F-4*

Lake Michigan, G-3
Lake Nipigon, D-2
Lake Nipissing, F-5*
Lake-of-the-Woods, D-1
Lake Ontario, G-5
Lake Panache, F-4*
Lake Rideau, F-6*
Lake St. Clair, G-4*
Lake Superior, E-2
Lansdowne House, C-3
London, G-4*
Longlac, D-3
Magnetawan River, F-4*
Mammamattawa, D-3
Manitoulin Island, F-4*
Mattawa, F-5*
Mattawa Wild
   River Park, F-5*
Midland, F-5*
Montreal, F-6*
Moose Factory, D-4
Moose River, D-4
Moosonee, D-4
Mt. Forest, G-4*
Muskoka Lakes, F-5*
Nakina, D-3
Niagara Falls, G-5*
Niagara Peninsula, G-5*
Niagara River, G-5*
Nipigon, D-2
North Bay, F-5*
Oba, D-3
Ogaki, C-3
Orillia, F-5*
Oshawa, G-5*
Ottawa, F-6*

Ottawa River, F-5*
Owen Sound, F-4*
Pagwa River, D-3
Parry Sound, F-4*
Pembroke, F-5*
Perth, F-6*
Peterborough, F-5*
Pickle Lake, C-2
Polar Bear
   Provincial Park, B-4
Port Colborne, G-5*
Port Hope, G-5*
Pukaskwa
   National Park, E-3
Queenston, G-5
Quetico
   Provincial Park, E-2
Rainy Lake, D-1
Rainy River (river), D-1
Rainy River (town), D-1
Red Lake, D-1
Renfrew, F-6*
Richmond Hill, G-5*
Rideau River
   and Canal, F-6*
Sarnia, G-4*
Sault Ste. Marie, F-3*
Savant Lake, D-2
St. Catharines, G-5*
St. Clair River, G-4*
St. Lawrence
   Lowlands, F-6*
St. Lawrence River
   and Seaway, F-6*
St. Marys River, F-3*
St. Thomas, G-4*

Severn River, B-2, F-5*
Shelburne, G-4*
Simcoe, G-5*
Sioux Lookout, D-1
Sleeping Giant
   Peninsula, E-2
Smiths Falls, F-6*
Smoky Falls, D-4
Stratford, G-4*
Sudbury, E-4*
Sudbury Basin, F-4*
Sundridge, F-5*
Terrace Bay, E-3
Thames River, G-4*
Thunder Bay, E-2
Timigami Provincial
   Forest, E-4
Timmins, E-4
Tobermory, F-4*
Toronto, G-5*
Trans-Canada
   Highway, D-2, F-5*
Trent River
   and Canal, F-5*
Trenton, F-5*
Uchi Lake, D-1
Upsala, D-2
Waterloo, G-4*
Wawa, E-3
Welland, G-5*
Welland Canal, G-5*
White River, E-3
Wiarton, F-4*
Windsor, G-4*
Winisk, B-3
Winisk River, C-3

Ontario is the second largest of Canada's provinces, with 412,582 square miles, nearly twice the size of Texas. It stretches 1,000 miles from east to west, and slightly more from north to south. The arrowhead of southern Ontario plunges south to the latitude of northern California. Neither roads nor railways penetrate the little-known northwest.

The province has a very irregular shape. Its only straight lines border Manitoba on the west and Quebec on the east. The southern border is carved by lakes and rivers. On the north, the salt waters of James Bay and Hudson Bay lap its shores.

Most of Ontario is rocky, part of the Canadian Shield. This collar of ancient rock around Hudson Bay covers the province from east to west, crowding south almost to the St. Lawrence River. It is covered with forest and dotted with lakes full of fish.

A rim of low swampy land to the north is called the Hudson Bay Lowlands. Some day it may grow hardy crops. At present it is bush and muskeg, threaded with many rivers.

The St. Lawrence Lowlands lie far to the south. A narrow strip of land beside the river widens into southern Ontario. This peninsula is rich farmland, the most valuable in Canada.

WATER, WATER EVERYWHERE

Rock and farmland are both precious to Ontario. Both were shaped by at least four Ice Ages.

Eons after the turmoil of creation filled the rocks with minerals, glaciers crawled south from the Arctic. The immense weight of ice scraped over the bedrock, pushing earth and stones ahead like a bulldozer.

Finally the ice melted, leaving huge lakes of fresh water. Stones and soil sank to the bottom. These glacial lakes shrank, exposing the fertile silt of the St. Lawrence Lowlands.

The St. Lawrence River Thousand Islands area.

Ontario is freckled with large and small lakes, inland from the Great Lakes. Some people claim there are a million, but less than half have names. Lake Nipigon, above Lake Superior, is nearly large enough to be counted a great lake. Lac Seul is only one of the many vast lakes in the northwest. In southern Ontario, the Rideau, Kawartha, and Muskoka lakes form three mazes of water.

Ontario is also a land of great rivers, with the Ottawa and St. Lawrence forming the southeastern borders. Both were highways of water for fur traders and explorers.

Immense rivers flow through northern Ontario, where Indians still canoe to the trading posts. The Moose River gathers its big tributaries to reach tidewater at Moose Factory on James Bay. The mighty Albany drains large lakes and innumerable streams as it crosses the District of Kenora. The Severn winds six hundred miles to meet salt water at Hudson Bay.

A VARIABLE CLIMATE

Covering such distances, Ontario has a great range of weather. Blossom Sunday comes to the Niagara Peninsula in May. At the same time, the animals of Polar Bear Park on Hudson Bay are waking from their winter sleep. Crops and gardens are planted in southern Ontario long before snowdrifts vanish from northern forests.

Cold winds from Hudson Bay bring snow and shivers. Warm winds from the south bring spring flowers and summer heat waves. Clammy winds from the east drop rain from cloudy skies. Best of all is the strong west wind, whipping across the lakes and blowing the skies clean of smog.

The weather varies greatly. A day that begins cloudy may be dazzling by noon. In fall, sunny mornings often end with an overcast sky. Ontario people say, "If you don't like the weather, just wait a bit. It will change."

Seasons are sharply marked. Winter may linger with its dirty snowdrifts—then suddenly it's spring. Summer comes with a rush and goes out gently. "Indian Summer"comes after the first snowflakes, a calm, lovely autumn when poplars turn yellow in the north, and maples redden in the south.

The large bodies of water to the north and south temper the heat of the summer and the cold of winter, though raw winds off Lake Ontario can make Toronto extremely uncomfortable in winter.

The snow can't come too early or last too long for some people. Farmers like snow lying on their bare fields. It keeps the soil from blowing away, and the meltwater seeps into the ground. Organizers of winter carnivals need cold weather. Even in February, however, there's no guarantee that there will be enough snow on the ground. At that time of the year, warm winds meeting arctic winds may create a thunderstorm that melts all the snow. The same conditions could as easily bring a snowfall heavy enough to block all roads.

The Indians of Ontario had a name for each month. The Moon of Falling Leaves might be September in the north and October in the south. The Moon of Returning Birds came earlier in the south than in the north. To the Cree Indians of James Bay, September was the month of The Moon when Deer Rub their Antlers, October was The Migrating Moon, December The Frosty Moon. They called May the month of The Mating Moon.

Four Children of Ontario

IAN OF BARRIE

This was the best summer Ian ever remembered. He went to scout camp for two weeks *and* he took a motor trip with his parents to Nova Scotia.

The family came to Canada from Scotland two years ago, and Ian's father found a job at once. He is an optometrist, and went to work for a large company that manufactures eyeglasses in Toronto. He thought he would have to stick at whatever job he took, but he learned that Canadians change their line of work easily. "There's a lot of opportunity here," he told Ian. "I might even start up a business of my own."

Two weeks of Ian's summer were spent at scout camp, where he learned a great deal about outdoor living and made many new friends.

21

The family lived in three rooms at first, and Ian's mother became a supply teacher. His parents had expected Canada to be much like Scotland, only bigger. They were surprised to find so many of their neighbors were from Asian and European countries, from Australia and Africa.

"Everybody is a minority race here," Ian told his parents after his first day of school. "We've got pupils from fifty-three different homelands, teacher said. So nobody can make fun of my red hair or the Indians' dark skins, or the way the Portuguese kids speak English."

Ian's father kept a sharp lookout for opportunities in his line of work. After a few months, he found an optometrist in Barrie who was ready to retire. The family moved to the busy little city north of Toronto and rented a house in a suburb. The houses on the street are much alike, and each has a big yard where children can play. Ian's parents have set up an outdoor grill and they picnic outside whenever the weather is nice. Ian's mother now teaches school full time.

The public school Ian attends is a large, modern building with a learning resources center. Ian is excited to find books and magazines, films and tape recordings, all of which he can use himself.

Students can decide which courses they want to take and what hobbies they want to pursue in special groups after school. Photography? Creative writing? Playacting? Ian chose sports, and is learning to play football and baseball, which he considers less exciting than soccer. In winter he belongs to a junior curling group. Curling is a Scottish game in which a team hurls big, round kettlestones down a lane of ice. Ian also likes the Boy Scouts, and has earned a badge for each new skill he has mastered.

Although Barrie is on a large bay, Ian lives a long way from the water. His home is close to the big highway that runs north from Toronto to Northern Ontario. This summer, Ian followed that road to Boy Scout camp in Algonquin Park. He paddled a canoe for the first time. As he grows older, he will make long canoe trips with the older Scouts.

Then the family loaded up the camper and drove east to explore Nova Scotia. Sometime they will go back to Scotland to visit their relatives, but only after they have seen more of their new country.

Ian hasn't decided what he wants to be when he grows up. Right now, he would like to run a summer resort for children or a hotel for tourists. His father reminds him, "You don't have to make up your mind just yet. Learn all you can, then decide for yourself. And remember that you can switch from one career to another in this country."

GLORIA OF FORT WILLIAM INDIAN RESERVE

When Gloria tried out her first pair of skis on the practice slopes of Mount McKay, she fell flat on her face. "Don't give up," called a young white man from the city. He helped her to her feet. "Someday you will ski right from the top!" As he left, he asked, "Where else in Ontario can you ski downhill for more than a mile?"

Gloria was too shy to speak. She raised dark eyes to the flat top a thousand feet above her, and smiled. She wishes she had told him that this is the mountain where Thunderbird had his nest long ago. The ski lodge below has a lovely mural of Thunderbird, painted by an artistic member of the Fort William Ojibway band. The village of frame houses is beyond the ski lift. Gloria's home is freshly painted a pale green.

From the slope, Gloria can look north to the city of Thunder Bay on the northern boundary of the reserve. Out in front, to the east, is the magnificent harbor formed by a long peninsula that looks like a huge figure lying asleep. Gloria almost believes that the Sleeping Giant is really Nanabozho, the great spirit who saved the animals from the Flood, according to Ojibway legend.

Gloria's mother is an active member of the Ontario Indian Association. She knows the band's history and says, "We in the Fort William Reserve are better off than most Indian bands. We have regained pride in our Indian heritage through making an effort."

She says that this band of Ojibway moved across the border from the United States in 1801. There they were called Chippewas, which sounds almost the same. They wanted to be near the fur trading post of Fort William, since most were trappers. They liked the mountain with two lakes on its flat top, the winding Kaministiquia River full of fish, the sandy beaches and coves of Lake Superior, and the maple forest.

Then in 1849, the Ojibway band signed a treaty by which they became absolute owners of thirty square miles. They sold some valuable land beside the river in 1905, but had fourteen thousand acres left, plenty for their village. Still, this land was not very good for crops, and not nearly big enough for hunting and trapping.

"But it turns out that this is very valuable property," Gloria's father reminds her. "This band doesn't need welfare."

The band got into the tourist business a few years ago by using part of its land for a trailer park and campground. Gloria's father is a caretaker, and is proud that the campground had to be expanded because of so much business. An uncle of Gloria's is in charge of the maple bush which produces delicious maple syrup and maple sugar candy, which tourists buy eagerly. Profits are shared among the members of the band.

About seventy families live on the reserve, and most of the men and girls work in the city. Some teach school. Some work at the grain elevators, or in the big railway yards, or on the docks. A quarter of the band members live in the city of Thunder Bay, which used to be the twin cities of Fort William and Port Arthur.

Gloria's home at the Fort William Indian Reserve is
not far from the beautiful High Falls at Thunder Bay.

Sometimes Gloria visits her relatives in the city, and they pass the
high school where her brother goes by bus each day. Gloria is eager
to get to high school, but is a little timid, too. When her relatives visit
the reserve they always say, "It's so nice here!" Gloria can't
understand why they don't move back.

Since the campground and sugarbush projects proved successful,
the young men of the band determined to go further and cut
snowmobile trails through the forest. They bought out the ski club
which had rented Indian property. The club has seventeen hundred
members, mostly white people. Gloria is proud of her cousin, who
manages the resort. Another young man from the village studies
business administration in Centennial College, and plays the violin
in the symphony orchestra.

It was young men like these who persuaded the federal and
provincial governments to give grants which made the projects
possible. They proved that an Indian band could not only plan a
good future, but carry those plans through to completion.

CECILE OF OTTAWA

Cecile guided her bicycle into the elevator of the tall brick apartment block where she lives in Ottawa. She doesn't trust the storage space in the basement, but parks her bike on the balcony of the family's sixth floor apartment. Pierre's bicycle is already there, because his school is closer to home. The convent school Cecile attends is ten blocks away.

Their mother was just putting away her paints and paper. She paints beautiful scrolls with fancy lettering like the monks used to do long ago. These are for presentation to important people. Cecile said in French, "Our class went to the Parliament Buildings today. Oh, the carvings in stone and marble are wonderful! A man was working up near the ceiling, chiseling out a figure. That's what I'd like to do someday. Or else make stained glass windows."

In school, Cecile and Pierre have their lessons in both French and English, and the whole family is bilingual. Cecile's father is a translator. He translates English writings into French for a government department. When he had an operation last winter, he fretted about not getting his work done in time for the publication date.

The street on which they live runs up to Parliament Hill where the main government buildings stand. Cecile thinks they are beautiful, all of stone and with pointed towers like old buildings in France.

Her father took her up to the top of the Peace Tower once, and she could see all the city and across the Ottawa River into the Province of Quebec. She looked for the blue roof of Grandmere's house in Hull, where she goes every Sunday afternoon. Beyond are the Laurentian Mountains where the family has a summer cottage beside a small lake.

Over to one side, Cecile could see the open market of Bytown Market, where her mother likes to buy fresh vegetables and eggs from the farmers. She usually shops in the plaza near home. Cecile likes to go with her mother to the market in the car.

From the tower, Cecile saw two streams flowing through the city. One was the Rideau River which falls into the Ottawa River like a curtain, which is what the French word *rideau* means. The other was the Rideau Canal, which reaches from the Ottawa River all the way to Kingston on Lake Ontario. There are eight locks in the canal right below the Peace Tower.

The tree-lined canal is beautiful at any time of year, but especially in summer when the flower beds are in bloom. Cecile likes it best in winter when the water is frozen and city workmen clear away the snow so people can skate. Cecile and her friends skate several miles in one direction before turning back. Pierre would rather play hockey on the school rink.

This section of the Rideau Canal system is a familiar Ottawa sight to Cecile, who ice skates near here in the winter when the canal is frozen.

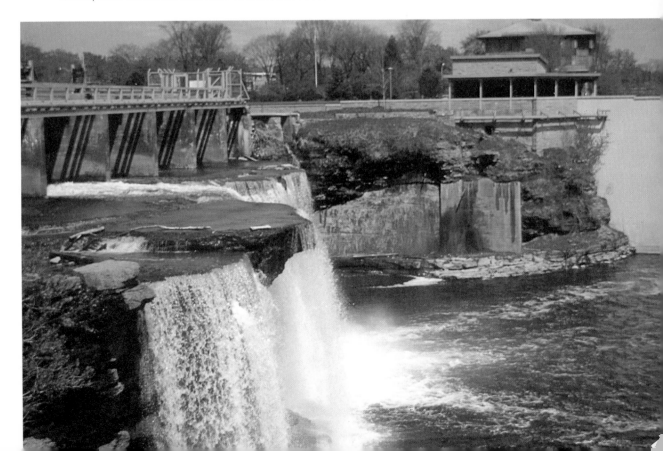

Christmas is the very best time of year, Cecile thinks. In school they make decorations, learn old French carols, and put on a costume play. The nuns choose the most artistic pupils to arrange the creche, or nativity scene. Cecile helped last year, and has plans to make the creche even more beautiful next year.

She looks forward to the time when she will be grown up enough to attend Midnight Mass. The church choir sings especially well then. Her Tante Gabrielle plays the organ, and her mother, as a member of the Altar Guild, helps decorate the church.

After Midnight Mass, Pierre and Cecile are wakened for *Reveillon*, the party at Grandmere's house in Hull. All the relatives are there, everyone is excited, telling stories and laughing. Someone starts a song, and Cecile is proud of how her father's deep bass harmonizes with her cousins' tenor voices. Still, they are used to singing together, and sometimes even put on a concert. Cecile never remembers much about the drive home through the winter darkness. She is so sleepy that the Christmas lights on the streets and buildings seem like just a lovely blur to her.

STEVE OF NIAGARA PENINSULA

The yellow school bus dropped Steve off at the entrance of a long drive. As he walked toward the yellow stuccoed house, he noticed that the big lawn needed cutting. That is his job, and he likes riding the new motorized lawnmower. His mother looked up from weeding the flower beds, and smiled. "There's milk in the fridge and cookies on the counter," she said in Ukrainian. "Then your father wants you to help in the packing shed."

Steve nodded. When you run a truck garden, everything else has to wait. He will cut the grass tomorrow, he decided as he nibbled at his cookies and gulped down two glasses of milk in the bright, modern kitchen. Everybody works hard on the family truck garden outside the city of St. Catharines on Niagara Peninsula. His mother does the bookkeeping, his older brother Michael keeps the machinery in running order, and his father is busy from early morning on, directing the work crew. Steve is a third-generation Canadian of Ukrainian origin.

"We're a farming family," his father always says. "Your grandfather came here from the Ukraine with only the clothes on his back and fifteen cents in his pocket. He worked as a hired man, saved his wages, then bought a few acres. We boys worked hard for him and he helped us all get started on land of our own, just as I will help Michael and you in turn."

Steve is not sure he wants to be a truck gardener. He has listened to his father grumbling about getting field workers, about shortages of baskets and crates just when you need them, about getting vegetables and berries to market at exactly the right time, about the problems of storing vegetables through the winter. Perhaps he should get a job like his married sister has. She works in a greenhouse for the Niagara Parks Commission.

There would be more money and less worry in working at the papermill in Thorold, or a factory in Welland. He wonders what it would be like to be a sailor on the Great Lakes. He sees the freighters moving up and down the Welland Canal that cuts across the Niagara Peninsula, carrying all kinds of cargoes, sometimes with lots of shiny, new cars on deck. Or he might go into politics, as many Ukrainian Canadians do.

During the school vacation in March, Steve's parents take a winter holiday before the rush of spring planting. Steve goes with them to Florida, the West Indies, or Mexico. It does not interfere with Easter, which Steve's mother would never allow. She is an active member of the Ukrainian Women's Association of Canada, and likes to keep up the old traditions. "We don't want to forget our language; it often comes in handy," she says.

Steve and his family celebrate two Easters and two Christmases. The Greek Orthodox Church to which they belong celebrates the holy days according to a different calendar, at least a week later than the ordinary calendar. Holy Week is a very solemn occasion, followed by Easter Sunday, a day of rejoicing and feasting on roast lamb.

On December 25, the family gifts lie on wheat straw under a Christmas tree, ready for opening before the turkey dinner. Steve has never believed in Santa Claus because he has always made presents for his family. He helps decorate the tree with garlands of paper loops and ties red apples to the branches. Special ornaments, such as gilded walnut shells and lovely snowflakes made from fine wire, are saved from one Christmas to the next. "It is good to keep our crafts alive," his mother says. "Our traditions become part of Canada's traditions."

The real Christmas comes on January 7, a religious holiday. On the night before, the whole family gathers at Steve's home. His mother wears her Ukrainian costume of bouncy petticoats, ribbons and flowers, and high boots. Steve watches at the window for the first star, then announces, "Christ is born!" The family sits down to a traditional dinner of twelve meatless dishes, one for each of the twelve apostles. It is the beginning of two weeks of gaiety, which ends with Ukrainian Independence Day, January 22. People go to big dinners, make long speeches, sing Ukrainian songs, and dance the polka. Steve is glad he can understand the speeches in Ukrainian, and is proud of the traditions his people have brought to Canada.

When Steve sees the freighters on the Welland Canal, he often wonders what it would be like to be a sailor on the Great Lakes.

The Indians of Ontario belonged to two great language groups, Algonkian and Iroquois. The Chippewa chief Wa-he-mah-wha-je-wabe, whose watercolor portrait was painted by William Armstrong, was an Algonkian-speaking Indian.

These Brantford area Indians, shown in another of William Armstrong's watercolors, were Iroquois-speaking Indians.

Ontario Yesterday

The land that is now Ontario belonged to Indians of two great language groups, Algonkian and Iroquois. Both groups were composed of several tribes, each with its own territory.

Algonkian-speaking Indians lived in forested country along the Ottawa River, Lake Huron, and Lake Superior. Iroquois-speaking tribes lived on both sides of Lake Erie and Lake Ontario. The largest tribe was the Huron, with about thirty thousand people.

THE FIRST FARMERS

These Iroquois tribes lived in stockaded villages of longhouses, narrow bark buildings holding a dozen or more families. No Indian owned house or land individually, but each village defended its territory vigorously.

Their land was fertile, and they had plenty of garden space. They cleverly planted the "three sisters" together—corn which grew straight

The Algonkian-speaking Indians lived in an area that was too cold and rocky to grow crops. They therefore lived by hunting and fishing, moving often to fresh areas. For their difficult winter travels, they developed the snowshoes and toboggans shown in this William Armstrong watercolor painted in 1878.

and tall, beans that climbed up the corn, and squash whose vines covered the ground between the corn plants. They knew how to preserve such food for winter.

The Iroquois tribes also used wild fruits and nuts. In spring they gathered sap from the maple trees and boiled it down to sugar in clay pots. Bees provided honey. Deer and moose roamed the forests; the rivers were full of salmon and the lakes full of trout.

Eventually the Iroquois tribes in what is now New York State felt crowded. They crossed the Niagara River into the territory of their relatives, in what is now Ontario. That always meant fighting. Though the invaders had fewer warriors, they were better organized. They usually won the battles, and carried off prisoners. Captive women and children were adopted, but men were killed.

The Indians were very fond of children, and let them have their way. Boys played a great deal, especially games that trained their eyes

The Algonkian-speaking Indians also used birchbark or deerhide to build easily movable wigwams and made birchbark canoes for easy summer travel.

and muscles. In summer, they played a vigorous ball game called lacrosse; in winter, they played hockey on frozen ponds, using a curved branch for a stick.

THE ALGONKIANS HUNTED TO LIVE

The land of the Algonkian-speaking tribes was too cold and rocky to grow crops. These tribes lived by hunting and fishing. They gathered wild food such as mushrooms, wild rice, birds' eggs, and frogs. Each family lived in a wigwam of birchbark or deerhide, a house that could easily be moved to new fishing and hunting areas.

Because they had to move often, the Algonkian-speaking tribes were inventive. They developed snowshoes and toboggans for winter travel, and birchbark canoes for summer. They cooked meat in watertight birchbark boxes by dropping hot stones into the water.

THE ENGLISH ARRIVE

The Indians who lived beside Hudson and James bays were astonished in 1610 when they saw a sailing ship in their waters. They called it "a great canoe with white wings."

It was the *Discovery*, captained by Henry Hudson, who was seeking a route to China. The ship had sailed through Hudson Strait, then turned south into the great sea of Hudson Bay.

The Englishmen found low, muddy shores and endless dark spruce forests. After a bitter winter on the shore of James Bay, the hungry, frightened crew mutinied. They set Hudson adrift, along with his son and some loyal sailors. The castaways died, but only a few mutineers lived to work the ship back to England.

More Englishmen followed, exploring Ontario's tidewater shores. They found only wilderness, with many large rivers. Pierre Radisson, the French-Canadian trapper-explorer, sold the English information about the "fur country." The Hudson's Bay Company, formed in 1670, built trading posts at the river mouths. Each summer, the company ships brought cargoes of hardware, cloth, tea, and sugar. These were traded to the Indians in exchange for beaver skins.

THE FRENCH GO SOUTH

French explorers had tried to reach China by a southern route up the St. Lawrence River. Samuel de Champlain, governor of New France, pushed past the rapids of the Ottawa River in 1613.

He had sent young men out from Quebec to explore the wilderness and make friends with the Indians. One was Etienne Brule, the first white man to see four of the Great Lakes. Brule took up Indian ways and became a valued interpreter and scout. Unfortunately, he quarreled with Champlain, with the missionary priests, and finally with the Huron Indians, who then killed and ate him.

Champlain was eager to convert the Indians to Christianity. French priests sacrificed comfort and safety to live in the wilderness, often in an Indian longhouse. They built three log missions at the foot of Georgian Bay, the largest being Ste. Marie-among-the-Hurons.

No one realized that the Europeans would bring new diseases to the Indians in the bush and in settlements. Having no natural immunity, the Huron Indians died of flu, measles, and smallpox. By 1640, only twelve thousand survived.

Their Iroquois relatives swept north with a few muskets obtained from New England traders. They plundered and burned, killed Indians and martyred five priests. The survivors fled to Quebec.

The land between the lakes was practically empty.

Fur trading almost stopped, since it was dangerous to travel. The governors of New France sent soldiers against the Iroquois tribes to destroy their villages and crops. Later they made peace, and the fur trade began again.

Governor Frontenac in 1673 built a strong outpost above the fierce rapids of the St. Lawrence, on the site of Kingston, Ontario. Another post rose at the mouth of the Humber River, where Toronto now stands. A fortification went up at Niagara, and another at Detroit.

The chief route of the fur traders led up the Ottawa River and into Lakes Huron and Superior. Once a year, fleets of thirty-six-foot canoes went west loaded with food, brandy, trade goods, and money to pay the garrisons at trading posts. Smaller canoes loaded with bales of fur met the big canoes at Thunder Bay.

The crews exchanged their loads. After a riotous party, they hurried back over the waterways before the rivers froze.

This pattern of fur trading continued after New France became British in 1763. Scots, Americans, and Englishmen became the new lords of the fur trade. They wanted the land west of the Ottawa River left to the Indians and the fur trade.

ONTARIO TAKES SHAPE

When the War of Independence began in 1775, many colonists remained loyal to England. Some Loyalists in New York State moved across the Niagara River at once. Others waited until the war ended.

More than six thousand United Empire Loyalists moved north into the region that became Ontario. It was then the western part of the long, narrow Province of Quebec. Only a few Indian bands lived there.

The British government bought land for the Loyalists from the Indians. Today the prices paid seem incredibly low, but they were unusually fair for that time.

Most of the Loyalists who came to Ontario crossed the St. Lawrence, and hewed farms out of the forest near Kingston. Those who crossed at Niagara tilled the rich orchard lands of the Niagara Peninsula. French settlers moved across the Detroit River into British North America.

PIONEER LIFE

These were the first white people to settle what is now Ontario. The land was covered with trees that shut out the sunlight, kept the ground wet, held the snow too long. The settlers had to make clearings in the bush in order to plant crops. The British government supplied food, tools, and seeds.

Loyalists from the American colonies knew how to handle pioneer tasks. They cut trees, built log cabins, and planted grain between the stumps. The next year, they pried out the great roots, and teams of oxen dragged them aside to serve as fences.

Life was hard, for the settlers had to create nearly everything they used, including furniture. They grew grain for themselves and their livestock. They made butter and cheese and candles, and preserved eggs and other foods for winter. They sheared their sheep, spun the wool into yarn, wove it into cloth, then used the cloth for blankets, curtains, and clothing.

Other settlers were almost helpless in the backwoods. They were the families of British soldiers and farmers from the British Isles who were used to a different life. Still, they helped each other, especially at "working bees." These were social events to which the women brought all the food they could spare, while the men put up a barn or house or cleared some land.

A PROVINCE OF THEIR OWN

Almost at once, these colonists asked for a separate province. They didn't like being ruled by a governor located in Quebec City. They wanted a colony in which English-speaking people could live by English laws and customs.

Thus, in 1791, the Province of Quebec was divided into two colonies. The higher land west of the Ottawa River was named Upper Canada; the land downriver along the St. Lawrence was called Lower Canada. Today we know them as Ontario and Quebec provinces.

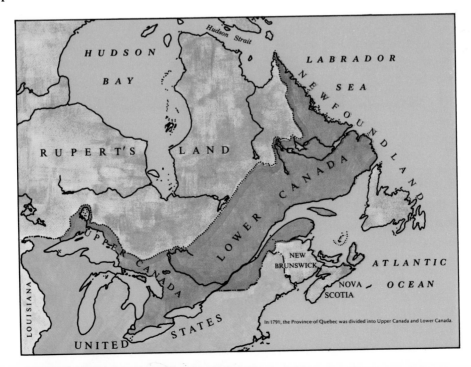

In 1791, the Province of Quebec was divided into Upper Canada and Lower Canada.

Colonel John Graves Simcoe, the first governor of Upper Canada.

Upper Canada got its first governor the following year, when Colonel John Graves Simcoe arrived. For the next four years, Governor Simcoe worked hard, bustling around on horseback and sailing ships. The colony especially needed a government and a capital, roads for defense and trade, and a land act.

Simcoe set up the usual colonial government. He chose a Legislative Council to advise him, and a Legislative Assembly was elected by the voters. He had the land surveyed, reserving some for the Indians, some for the government, some for the support of the church.

The governor would have liked the capital to be Newark, now Niagara-on-the-Lake. But that was too close to the American border. London was well inland, but not central enough. Toronto, his third choice, was central, halfway between Montreal and Windsor. Though the shores were marshy, the old fur trading site had an excellent harbor on Lake Ontario. Simcoe made it a military and naval base, with star-shaped Fort York to guard the settlement he named York. He didn't like the Indian name, Toronto, meaning "a place of meeting."

Simcoe's roads, meant for moving soldiers quickly, were a great help to business. Settlements grew. Simcoe advertised for more settlers from the British Isles and the United States. Thousands of immigrants poured into Upper Canada to take up free land.

TROUBLE ON THE BORDER

The American settlers outnumbered British immigrants and Loyalists. They were not fully trusted by either, and their loyalty to Upper Canada was soon tested in the War of 1812.

In Washington, President Madison declared it was "manifest destiny" that the continent must become the United States of America. He decided to invade the provinces to the north. The British army, the Indians, and the new settlers resisted.

Forts on both sides of the border were captured and recaptured. Generals of both armies showed courage or retreated in fear. American ships won a naval victory on Lake Erie, as British ships did on Lake Ontario. American troops burned farmhouses on Niagara

Peninsula. Canadian defenders promptly burned houses on the American side of the river. Americans captured Fort York and burned the government buildings. In turn, British troops invaded Washington and set fire to the White House.

Few people wanted this war, and it ended on Christmas Eve, 1814. Neither side won. But the Americans did not take British North America, and the provinces were proud of that. Yet the treaty gave the United States extra territory west of Lake Superior.

All parties agreed to keep warships off the Great Lakes. Still, Upper Canada worried that the United States might attack again. The colony built more roads and canals away from the border. But the peace was real and lasting.

REVOLUTION IN UPPER CANADA

Now the colonists had time to think about the hardships of pioneer life, and other grievances. They resented the arrogance of the Legislative Council, whom they called "the Family Compact" because most of its members were related.

They complained about the empty land reserved for the support of the Church of England clergy. No one paid taxes on that land, and no one improved it by drainage or weed control. Worse, only these clergymen could perform marriage ceremonies, though less than half the Upper Canadians were Anglicans.

Methodist preachers trudged on bush trails or rode horseback over bumpy log roads to hold meetings in lonely farmhouses. Gradually they and the Roman Catholic priests were recognized as real ministers and allowed to carry out their religious duties.

A small, red-haired Scottish immigrant, William Lyon Mackenzie, took every complaint seriously. He wrote fiery, insulting editorials in a newspaper he started in 1824. Mackenzie considered himself a reformer. The Family Compact called him a dangerous radical. Three times he was elected to the Legislative Assembly, and three times he was thrown out for his insulting remarks. Yet he was voted in as the first mayor of Toronto, when the settlement of York became a town in 1834, and took its old name.

By 1837, Mackenzie had roused men to the point of action. Some were hotheads. Most were deeply troubled about the future of the province. In December, some five hundred men gathered outside Toronto, armed with a few muskets and pitchforks. When they met a troop of regular soldiers, a few shots were fired—out of range—and the rebels took to their heels.

The "revolution" was put down in five days, and Mackenzie fled to the United States. A few rebels were hanged, a few transported to a convict colony in Australia. Most were pardoned. Thirteen years later, Mackenzie returned to Toronto to find things changed. His revolution had not failed completely.

The Mackenzie Rebellion had forced the British government to think seriously. A special commissioner, Lord Durham, had come out to learn what was troubling the Canadians of Upper and Lower Canada.

Lord Durham talked with the Family Compact and with reformers, farmers, and merchants. The Durham Report warned that the colonists must be given more control over their own affairs. Otherwise they would be lost, as were the American colonies.

COLONY INTO COUNTRY

Lord Durham believed the provinces of British North America should unite into a single country. Upper and Lower Canada agreed to try a union. In 1841, they became the United Provinces of Canada, Canada West and Canada East, now Ontario and Quebec.

Kingston, the commercial hub of Canada West, became the capital for the first four years. Then it was the turn of French-speaking

Montreal, the business center of Canada East. After that, the government sat in Toronto and Quebec City every two years. It was very unsatisfactory.

In 1857, the United Provinces asked Queen Victoria to choose a permanent capital. The Queen studied the map, and put her finger on a small lumbering town far from the jealous cities. "Ottawa shall be your capital," said she.

Gradually the idea of a united country spread east and west. The provincial premiers held a meeting in Prince Edward Island in 1864, followed by meetings in other cities. Four provinces decided to federate, and on July 1, 1867, they became the Dominion of Canada. The other provinces joined the confederation later.

Canada West changed its name for the last time. It took the name Ontario, an Indian word meaning "a very pretty lake."

Ontario's boundaries then included all of southern Ontario and a strip above Lake Superior. To the north and west was Rupert's Land, administered by the Hudson's Bay Company. Gradually Ontario expanded westward to its present border with Manitoba, and northward to Hudson Bay. By 1912, it had reached its present size.

The people of Ontario felt that their province was wonderfully progressive. Its industries and agriculture were growing. Its population was the largest of the provinces, and immigration helped it increase yearly.

That changed suddenly with the outbreak of World War I in Europe. Ontario, along with the rest of Canada, went into battle beside Great Britain. Many thousands of soldiers died or were wounded, and every town raised its war memorial.

Ontario also helped the war effort by raising food for the armies and by making munitions. For the first time, women worked beside men in the fields, offices, and factories. When the war ended, Ontario had become an industrial rather than an agricultural province.

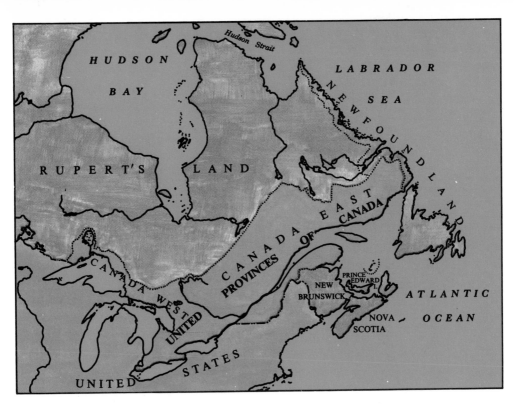

In 1841, Upper and Lower Canada became the United Provinces of Canada,
Canada West and Canada East (now Ontario and Quebec).
In 1867, four provinces federated to become the Dominion of Canada.
The other provinces joined the federation at later dates.

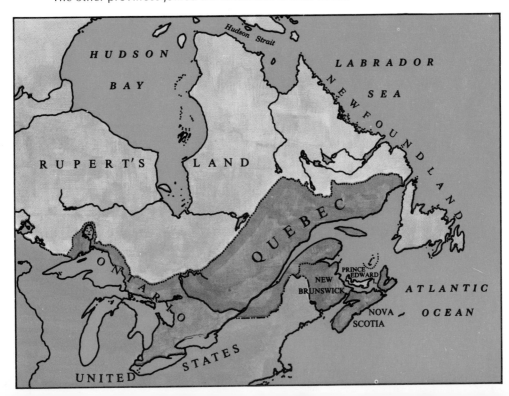

Ontario Today

Canadian government is much like that of England, with Queen Elizabeth as its head. As Queen of Canada, she is represented in Ottawa by a Canadian-born Governor General. He does not rule, but no bill passed in Parliament becomes law until he signs it. He presides at official functions such as the opening and closing of Parliament, and entertains the country's distinguished guests.

The Queen is also the head of each provincial government, where she is represented by a Lieutenant-Governor. In 1974, with the appointment of Pauline McGibbon, Ontario became the first province to name a woman to that position.

When the provinces confederated in 1867, each gave up some of its

Parliament Hill, Ottawa, is the home of the Canadian federal government.

47

power to the federal government, just as the states yielded some rights to Washington. Ottawa thus has authority over citizenship and immigration, relations with other countries, postal services, transportation, criminal law, and many other aspects of today's life.

The Province of Ontario is responsible for education, health, the growth of municipalities, roads, forests and mines, agriculture, civil law, and many more departments. There is a great deal of consultation among the premiers of the provinces and with the Prime Minister in Ottawa.

The federal government in Ottawa and the provincial government in Toronto are elected democratically. Whichever party wins the most seats forms the government. The party with the second largest number becomes the Opposition, whose duty it is to watch the government sharply. The government may hold office for any length of time up to five years.

Ontario is governed by the Provincial Parliament, sometimes called the Legislative Assembly. The members of a political party choose a leader who runs for a seat. The leader of the party that obtains the most seats becomes the premier. The premier then chooses his cabinet, or executive committee. The Minister of Health is responsible for everything in that Ministry, as another minister is responsible for the Ministry of Education.

A smaller area of government is the county in southern Ontario and the district in the north where there are fewer people. Governor Simcoe created the counties and gave them English names. London on the Thames River is the county seat of Middlesex. Many of the districts have Indian names, such as Nipissing. The largest is the District of Kenora, spreading all across the top of the province.

Smaller still is the municipal government, where voters elect a mayor or a reeve and a council. A city council is divided into committees. The Public Works Committee, for example, looks after paving streets, city architecture, garbage collection, snow removal, sewers, traffic, and much more.

Sometimes the province sets up a commission to handle special projects, such as the Ontario Health Commission or the Niagara Parks Commission. Its members are appointed by the government but operate independently.

The Ontario Hydro-Electric Power Commission is the largest public utility in Canada. It was established in 1906, when a small group of manufacturers banded together. They needed low-cost power for industry, but private plants at Niagara Falls charged high rates. Under Sir Adam Beck of London, Ontario, the dream grew to a multi-billion-dollar empire of 350 municipalities.

Ontario Hydro exports power to the United States, and its rates are still low. Electricity comes not only from many waterfalls and rapids, but also from plants where coal is burned to produce steam. Uranium from northern Ontario has proved very satisfactory in several nuclear reactors, and more are under construction.

SOCIAL LEGISLATION HELPS

Both the Canadian government and the Ontario government try to give everyone a chance to live well. Taxes pay for social services that aid all people.

A baby born in Ontario is immediately listed for Family Allowance benefits from the federal government. The monthly check grows with John or Mary to the age of eighteen, if they stay in school.

If John's father loses his job, he will be paid a weekly sum by the Unemployment Insurance Fund, to which he contributes each payday. John's grandmother began to receive the Old Age Pension when she reached sixty-five.

If Mary's father is injured on the job, the Workmen's Compensation pays part of his wages. If Mary needs an operation, most or all of the cost will be paid by the Ontario Hospital Insurance Plan to which her father contributes.

If John were crippled in an automobile accident—even if the drivers involved were uninsured—he would be covered by insurance, as there is a government fund to help victims of accidents caused by uninsured drivers.

Good health is very important to anyone's happiness. Regional health units began in Ontario in 1973, to make sure that no one who needs help is overlooked. This includes the doctors and nurses who look after children in the schools.

EDUCATION MATTERS

Ontario people have always taken a keen interest in education. In pioneer days, the Anglican Bishop John Strachan argued that education was for the upper class, the born leaders. That was his theory when he founded King's College in 1827, which grew into the University of Toronto.

"Education should be free to everyone," said Rev. Egerton Ryerson, a Methodist minister. After exploring educational systems in Europe, in 1846 Ryerson wrote his famous *Report*. This became the base of the public school system in Ontario. His goal of free general education was achieved in 1871. Today all children must go to school to the age of sixteen.

People still debate about education. For instance, are swimming pools and television sets "frills"? Should French-speaking students have to attend English-speaking schools? At present, teaching is carried on in French in twenty-nine Ontario high schools.

Ontario now has fifteen universities, of which the University of Toronto is oldest and largest. It is a federation of several colleges that were begun by religious groups but are now supported by taxes, tuition fees, and generous donations.

This university, like most, has strong links with the community. Student teachers train in Toronto schools, and medical students work

50

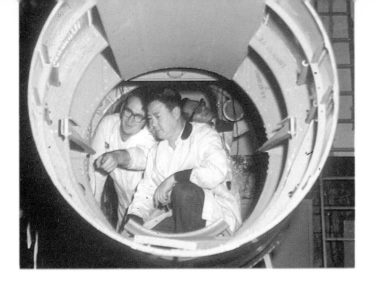

There are twenty community colleges of applied arts and science in Ontario. Students in these colleges take some classical subjects along with a variety of technical and vocational courses. Above: Airframe mechanics learn their trade at Centennial College. Right: Meat-cutting instruction at George Brown Community College. Below: Erindale College, part of the University of Toronto. Founded in 1827, the University of Toronto is Ontario's oldest and largest university.

in city hospitals. Library students fan out through the impressive library system, and students in many courses work in the Royal Ontario Museum. The University of Western Ontario, like the University of Toronto, is noted for its medical research laboratories.

Poverty need not keep a student out of a university. He can try for student loans, bursaries, or scholarships.

Enrollment at universities increased with war veterans. New courses were added at Toronto, Queen's, McMaster, and Western Ontario universities. Several colleges were upgraded to university status. New universities were built at St. Catharines, Waterloo, Sudbury, and Thunder Bay.

Because many young people preferred a technical education, there are now twenty community colleges of applied arts and science in the province. Students take some classical subjects along with a variety of courses from baking to undertaking.

Adult education goes on in universities and night schools. Waves of immigration called for instruction in speaking English.

Students in public and high schools have a wide choice in what subjects they will take. They may learn the creative arts of painting, music, drama, crafts, writing, and film making. Often groups of parents provide extra materials or equipment such as band instruments or cameras.

Education reaches to the Indian settlements of the far northern areas of the province. Some of the Indians have teachers; a few take correspondence courses. Some attend railway school, a railway coach fitted up as a classroom. There are five such coaches, moved from one siding to another so that every child gets some schooling.

TRANSPORTATION

Navigable waters and ports come under federal control. So do railways and airlines that cross provincial boundaries. Many operations are owned by the people, such as the Canadian Broadcasting Corporation, the Canadian National Railways, and Air Canada. They have privately owned competition in CTV, the Canadian television network, in the Canadian Pacific Railway, and Canadian Pacific Airline.

Ontario people make use of them all.

Railways are now more important for the freight they haul than for the passengers they carry. Strings of grain cars, often more than a hundred linked behind a diesel locomotive, roll eastward from the prairies to ports on the St. Lawrence Seaway. Westward they carry manufactured and processed goods such as clothing, cars, or steel pipes.

The Canadian Pacific Railway, completed in 1885, met almost as much trouble crossing northern Ontario as it did crossing the Rocky Mountains. The Canadian National is a combination of many lines, rescued from debt by the federal government. Both railways have many tracks in southern Ontario, and both arch north of Lake Superior on their way to the Pacific.

Two smaller lines are entirely in Ontario, one owned by the province, the other owned by shareholders. The Algoma Central Railway winds north from Sault Ste. Marie for three hundred miles through rugged mountain scenery. Its main freight is pulpwood for the papermill and concentrated iron ore for the steel plant, both at "the Soo." The Ontario Northland was built by the province to reach the Little and Great Clay Belts of northern Ontario. It, too, hauls pulp and minerals, as it shuttles between North Bay and Moosonee on James Bay.

All of these railways also own trucks, only some of Ontario's thousands of trucks and trailers. Some railway lines have stopped carrying passengers, since most people travel by car or bus. Southern Ontario is crisscrossed by main roads, country roads, and superhighways. Two long, lonely highways cross northern Ontario. One of these is the Trans-Canada Highway, opened in 1962.

Commercial shipping has used the Great Lakes ever since the days of the fur brigades. Canals were dug to bypass the rapids of the St. Lawrence River, the Gorge and Falls at Niagara, and the rapids of the St. Marys River at Sault Ste. Marie. Though these canals were large enough to carry most lake freighters, most seagoing vessels could not use them.

That changed with the opening of the St. Lawrence Seaway in 1959. This was the biggest undertaking in Canada's history, though shared with the United States. It has turned lakeports into seaports from Montreal to Thunder Bay—all along most of Ontario's southern border.

The section between Lakes Erie and Huron is said to be the busiest waterway in the world. Small canals have been deepened and widened to handle very large ships. Canal locks form steps of water to raise vessels 580 feet from sea level to the level of Lake Superior.

A freighter may carry a deckload of trucks the full 2,300-mile length of the Seaway, from the Atlantic to Thunder Bay at the head of Lake Superior. The ship unloads at the busy modern docks. It takes on a cargo of prairie wheat, or iron ore, or huge rolls of newsprint paper. Back it goes down the lanes and steps of water to its new destination.

North of the Seaway, the great rivers are still Indian highways. They are also used by prospectors, hunters, and surveyors in motor canoes. In winter the frozen rivers provide roadways for snowmobiles and tractor trains. The snowmobiles are used on the traplines in place of dogsleds. The tractors haul strings of big sleds filled with freight for trading posts.

The rivers provide landings for aircraft. The planes are equipped with skis in winter, with aluminum floats in summer. There are few airstrips to serve wheeled aircraft.

Some airline companies operate only in northern Ontario. They carry supplies to trading posts, and bring out loads of furs, mining concentrates, or frozen fish. They charter flights for prospectors and

Special government aircraft such as
the one above fight forest fires by
dumping thousands of gallons of water
onto the blazing trees of a forest fire.

trappers, hunters and fishermen. They bring sick people to the
hospital, or carry crews to a forest fire.

Special government aircraft, designed to help fight forest fires, are
equipped with great tanks. They fly low over a lake and scoop up
thousands of gallons of water. Then they swing up and dump the water
onto the blazing trees. This halts the fire, or puts it out.

In southern Ontario there are many scheduled flights out of airports
large and small. The largest is Toronto International Airport. It gets so
much traffic that a new airport will be needed soon.

Natural Treasures

Of all Ontario's natural treasures, the most important are clean air and water. Streams and rivers link countless lakes. Ontario is fortunate in having nearly fifty thousand square miles of fresh water.

The people of Ontario care a great deal about ecology. They make laws to prevent air pollution by industries and settlements, and water pollution by sewers or ships. Ontario and the five American states bordering on the Great Lakes are working together to clean up the waterways.

The most important need is pure water to drink. Farms and gardens need good water. Great quantities are used in commercial laundries, in car washing, and in the home, especially in the kitchen and bathroom. Industry uses even more in making paper and cooling metals. Water spins the turbines in most Ontario power plants to create electricity for homes and industries.

Water and forests are natural partners, and both create oxygen that purifies the air.

Ontario's forests cover many thousands of square miles
and turn the province into a blaze of color every autumn.

Trees need water to grow. In turn they hold the moisture in the
ground. In southern Ontario, the forests are mostly hardwoods such as
maple, birch, beech, and oak. Farther north grow the softwoods such as
poplar, basswood, and evergreens. Spruce forests cover many thousand
square miles.

The forests provide lumber for building houses and furniture,
baskets, boats, and many other things. Their highest money value is in
paper, manufactured from the fast-growing spruce and poplar trees.
The province has set aside forest reserves. Trees may be cut under
strict control, and the area reseeded.

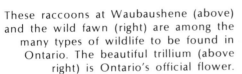

These raccoons at Waubaushene (above) and the wild fawn (right) are among the many types of wildlife to be found in Ontario. The beautiful trillium (above right) is Ontario's official flower.

KINDRED OF THE WILD

The waters and trees shelter and feed the wild creatures. The shy deer and the great moose roam here, the timber wolf and the fox. Where poplars grow, beavers build their dams to deepen the water around their lodges. Mink and otter find holes among the tree roots, and muskrats build their mounds in marshes. Black bears sleep in their dens through the winter; polar bears hunt seals in Hudson Bay.

All animals and birds are protected in the numerous national and provincial parks. Other large areas are kept as game sanctuaries. Here the animals are safe from hunters and trappers. Waterfowl refuges and bird sanctuaries are dotted throughout southern Ontario.

The muddy shores of Hudson Bay are home to millions of waterfowl which fly north each spring to breed. The gabble of wild geese in migration can be heard even in cities. Great whistling swans rest at Long Point in Lake Erie on their way to and from nesting grounds far to the north.

Almost 380 species of birds nest in Ontario. Ravens, gulls, and chickadees stay in Ontario all year round. Nature lovers feed bluejays, cardinals, and grosbeaks throughout the winter. Most birds return in spring, beginning with crows, robins, and warblers.

The birds delight the ear and eye and are the farmer's friends. Many birds live entirely on insects, while others eat weed seeds. Owls and hawks prey on destructive mice and rabbits.

TREASURE IN THE EARTH

Southern Ontario has some of the finest soil any farmer could wish. When the prehistoric glacial lakes shrank, they left fertile silt behind. Tobacco crops now grow on the ancient sandbars and the limestone reefs are covered with orchards. This precious land is only a small part of the province, though pockets of good earth do occur in the Canadian Shield near Sault Ste. Marie, Thunder Bay, and Rainy River, as well as in the two Clay Belts of northeastern Ontario.

Nature was generous to Ontario in minerals of many kinds. The Indians long ago dug copper beside Lake Huron and made knives of the soft metal. Indians beside Lake Superior knew of iron ore, but did not know how to smelt it. Indians of Thunder Bay told of the silver at the foot of the Sleeping Giant, which became Ontario's first silver mine.

Pioneer manufacturers found clay that was suitable for bricks and sewer pipes. They ground limestone into cement to pave their streets. They found salt near Windsor, and natural gas beside Lake Erie.

The Canada Goose (known to Canadians as "Honkers") is a familiar sight in Ontario, and the cries of the large flocks can be heard for miles around during the annual migration.
The Sudbury area (above) is the major producer of Ontario's copper and nickel.

Oil drillers with primitive rigs bored into the earth near Sarnia, and in 1858 produced what is believed to be North America's first oil well. Pumps still jog up and down in backyards, though the oil flow is small.

Ontario's glacier-scraped rocks are a mineral treasure chest not easy to unlock. Hardrock mining needs heavy machinery and large sums of money.

Human Treasures

Many Ontarians have become widely known for their skills. Some chose to remain in their province, while others found fame abroad.

Notable figures from the past include Joseph Brant, the Indian chieftain who came with the Loyalists to set up the Six Nations Reserve near Brantford; Pauline Johnson, the Mohawk princess whose poetry is still read and loved; and Paul Kane, the Irish-born artist of Toronto who left a priceless record of Canadian Indian life.

There was Sir William Osler, the great physician who revolutionized medical practice nearly a century ago. Dr. William Saunders, a London druggist, turned a gardening hobby into the crossbreeding of grain in Ottawa. He made it possible for farmers around the world to grow wheat much farther north. Adelaide Hoodless, a farmer's daughter near Hamilton, launched the biggest women's club, the Women's Institute.

Stephen Leacock's humorous sketches have been translated into a dozen languages. Lester Bowles Pearson, outstanding in international affairs and later Prime Minister, in 1957 was Canada's first winner of the Nobel Peace Prize.

When A. Y. Jackson died in 1974 at the age of ninety-one, he was the last of the original Group of Seven. These Toronto artists in 1920 rebelled against romantic landscapes. They saw beauty in the rugged Canadian countryside. They painted the rocks of northern Ontario in bold lines and strong colors. Some critics were shocked, but galleries now are proud to display the paintings of "A.Y." and his friends.

The home of Stephen Leacock, Canadian economist and humorist, has become an Orillia, Ontario tourist attraction.

Among musicians, Edward Johnson began his singing career at the age of five and became famous in Europe and as manager of the Metropolitan Opera Company of New York. Sir Ernest MacMillan was knighted for his services to music in Canada. His musical career spanned eight decades.

ON STAGE

Glenn Gould of Toronto has gathered awards at home, in the United States, and in Europe. His mother gave him piano lessons until, at ten, Glenn won his first scholarship. At twelve, he was the youngest pupil ever to graduate from the Royal Conservatory of Music. Glenn made his professional debut two years later, in 1946, with the Toronto Symphony Orchestra. He now prefers to record classical music rather than perform on the concert stage.

Canada's population is certainly large enough to support the performing arts. But it is so widely scattered that travel costs leave little profit. Most artists feel they must test their skills on larger audiences in the United States and Europe.

Concert singers such as soprano Lois Marshall, contralto Maureen Forrester, and lyric soprano Teresa Stratas perform abroad more often than they do in Ontario. Jan Rubes, bass, and Jon Vickers, tenor, have become famous in operatic circles.

Popular singers Gordon Lightfoot and Anne Murray maintain homes in Toronto, though most of their engagements are in the United States. Ontario-born Neil Young prefers California as the background for his highly original songs. Paul Anka began singing in Ottawa clubs when he was only twelve, and three years later, wrote and recorded his first big hit, *Diana*.

Some Ontario actors have become stars in Hollywood and New York. An older generation includes Mary Pickford, who began life as Gladys Smith of Toronto; Raymond Massey, of the Ontario manufacturing family; and Hume Cronyn of London, veteran of many stage plays. Lorne Greene of Ottawa, after a career in Canadian radio and on the New York stage, turned to television. His most popular role was Ben Cartwright of *Bonanza*, a television series shown in ninety countries.

Canadians think of themselves as sober-minded. Yet Ontario has produced comedians of repute. Johnny Wayne and Frank Shuster write their own hilarious skits. Don Harron created a caricature Parry Sound farmer well known on English and Canadian radio. Comedienne Barbara Hamilton commutes between Toronto and London, England, to work on stage and in films. Her favorite part was Marilla in the musical version of *Anne of Green Gables*.

Rich Little of Ottawa is a most successful mimic. His remarkable voice and memory can immediately produce any of 140 distinctive voices. Rich learned early that mimicking his high school teachers meant trouble. After being expelled, he got a job as a theater usher, and was soon giving impressions of the movie actors. Before long, he shocked and delighted Canadian audiences by spoofing politicians. His Hollywood nightclub audiences find his impressions of American politicians equally funny.

People in Stratford were aghast when young Tom Patterson proposed a festival of Shakespeare's plays. Who would come to a quiet Ontario town for drama? But Patterson persisted, and in 1953 a strange-shaped tent rose beside the Avon River. Sir Alec Guiness launched the festival in the role of Richard III.

Four years later a magnificent permanent Festival Theatre was opened. All of Shakespeare's major dramas have been presented, and the season has lengthened to five months. In winter, the company tours Canadian cities, and in spring has made some successful tours in Europe and Australia.

The Stratford Festival is one of the most respected in North America. Visitors come from all parts of Canada, from the United States, and in fact from every continent. Many bring picnic lunches to

The duel scene from Hamlet is enacted on the banks of the Avon River.
The Stratford Shakespearean Festival Theatre is in the background.

the park, where English swans accept bread crusts. When they are
not attending Festival programs, visitors may see Canadian plays and
concerts performed in other buildings in Stratford.

THE PRINTED PAGE

While most book publishers are located in Toronto, many Canadian
writers are published both abroad and at home. Popular novels of the
past include Ralph Connor's pioneer tales, Thomas Costain's historical
romances, and the Jalna series by Mazo de la Roche.

Thomas Costain of Brantford was a major Canadian magazine editor
before he became editor of the *Saturday Evening Post*. He wrote
excellent histories as well as fiction in his spare time. *The Black Rose*
and *The Silver Chalice* were both made into movies in Hollywood.

Mazo de la Roche of Toronto won a literary prize from a Boston publisher for her first book, *Jalna*. Though she preferred her other more serious writings, the public loved Jalna. She wrote sixteen books about the Whiteoaks family, all of them translated into many languages. They were recently filmed as a television series.

A more profound writer is Morley Callaghan of Toronto. His novels are about everyday people, written with great understanding. His short stories appear in many collections.

Ontario has produced many poets, none greater than E. J. Pratt of the epic verse. Outstanding today are Margaret Atwood and Al Purdy.

Ontario's most popular writers, Pierre Berton and Farley Mowat, are neither novelists nor poets. Berton was born in Yukon Territory. His book *Klondike*, tells the story of the Yukon gold rush. His two volumes on the Canadian Pacific Railway became bestsellers and the basis for a television series.

Farley Mowat amuses children and grownups with his exaggerations in *The Boat Who Wouldn't Float*. He rouses sympathy for wolves and whales, which he considers endangered species. Farley's northern books include *Sibir* and the prize-winning juvenile, *Lost in the Barrens*.

SPORTS

Ontario has produced winners such as golfers Ada MacKenzie and recently Marlene Streit. Barbara Ann Scott of Ottawa at sixteen became the youngest North American champion figure skater. In 1948, she brought Canada its first Olympic gold medal for figure skating. Radio bulletins in 1954 kept Canadians tense while sixteen-year-old Marilyn Bell of Toronto swam across Lake Ontario. She swam nearly forty miles through that cold water, the only woman ever to do so. In August, 1974, another schoolgirl of the same age, Cindy Nicholas, made the swim of thirty-two miles under perfect conditions in fifteen and a half hours.

A majority of the hockey players in the big American leagues are Canadian. The Toronto Maple Leafs play against men they knew on school rinks.

Bobby Orr of the Boston Bruins learned hockey from his father in Parry Sound, near Georgian Bay. Professional scouts discovered the speedy twelve-year-old in a playoff in 1961. Bobby reached training camp when he was barely seventeen.

By the time he was twenty-five, Bobby Orr had won more awards than most athletes win in a lifetime. Sports writers declared the defenseman of the Boston Bruins "the most accomplished and exciting hockey player of his generation." The coach of a rival team admitted, "He does everything just a little bit better than everybody else."

The People
Live in Ontario

Waves of immigrants have come to Canada for several reasons. Some hoped for a better life, some came to avoid military service, some came to escape persecution. Since World War II a steady flow has come from the British Isles, the United States, and Europe. Smaller numbers have arrived from the Caribbean, Africa, India, and China.

About half of the newcomers settled in Ontario, chiefly in the cities. Southern Ontario is the most densely populated province, with more than a third of Canada's people. A mixture of fifty different nationalities form Ontario's nearly eight million people.

Sudbury boasts of at least thirty nationalities. Finns and Poles work together in the mines. French live harmoniously with English. Ukrainians eat at Chinese cafes, and Scottish bank clerks accept American checks. They may all speak English with an accent, but their children do not.

Each July, a "Caravan" is held in Toronto, a festival of ethnic groups displaying their arts and skills. Books and newspapers in many languages are on exhibit. Ukrainian dancers wear gay beribboned costumes. Latvian choirs sing, and music is played on balalaika, sitar, and pipe.

Jamaicans and others from the West Indies hold an exciting "Caribana," a week-long carnival, on Toronto Islands each summer.

Toronto has more Italian-speaking citizens than most cities in Italy! Some arrived two generations ago, others between the wars. But the largest numbers came after 1945.

The Scots have been the strongest force in shaping the Ontario character—cautious, ambitious, and occasionally lively. The skirl of bagpipes is familiar across the province. It may be heard from a military band rehearsing in a local armory, or in a parade, or at the opening of a supermarket. Scottish lassies dance the reel and their brothers toss the caber at Highland games in several towns.

All these people brought their memories of the "Old Country" with them, traditions they handed down to their children. They brought their religious faiths, too.

The Scots have been one of the strongest forces in shaping the Ontario character. Below: The Highland Games in Fergus, Ontario.

RELIGION

The shining spires of Roman Catholic churches can be seen
alongside Anglican steeples throughout the province. Onion-shaped
towers of the Eastern Orthodox faith rise near the dome of a
synagogue or the storefront quarters of a small sect. The plain
meetinghouse of the Old Order Mennonites contrasts with the
modernistic architecture of a Lutheran church. Buddhist and Moslems
have temples in Toronto.

Many Japanese belong to the Buddhist faith. Most of the Japanese in
Ontario came from the British Columbia coast after 1945. They
have proved successful in professions as varied as gardening, law,
manufacturing, and teaching.

WHERE PEOPLE LIVE

Most of Ontario's people live in cities in the southern part of the
province. It is the place of opportunity, they believe, especially for
artists of all kinds. The big city has specialized schools and hospitals,
the most exciting entertainment, or the largest number of customers.

Life in the smaller cities is much the same. Children go to school
while their parents work. Many women work, and most fathers help
with the housework. They work a five-day week, and on Saturday the
whole family may go to the shopping center. On Sunday the family
may go to church in the morning, to a movie or picnic in the afternoon.

Most Ontario families still live in separate houses with lawns and
flowerbeds. Housing developments in big cities are usually
apartment blocks, and they are increasing in smaller towns, too. It is
hard to get help to put on storm windows or tend the furnace.
Apartment living is easier, though more expensive.

Even farmhouses are changing. The big houses of the past are not
needed and they are hard to heat. New small houses are serviced with

electricity, have an oil furnace, and a full bathroom. The radio in the kitchen and television in the living room do away with the old isolation.

Every farm has at least one car or a light truck for trips to town. School buses pick up the children and carry them to central schools. County bookmobiles supply the latest books at regular stops.

Rural slums do exist, often near old mines or lumber mills. Temporary shacks continue in use, but their owners have lost pride. Eventually these places become ghost towns, abandoned by everyone.

Nowadays the government insists on a town plan. If a mine develops, the people must have decent houses to live in. One example of an "instant town" is Elliot Lake, east of Sault Ste. Marie. As the uranium mines came into production, work began on a model community. The Ontario government built houses, schools, churches, hotels, and a shopping mall, ready for people to use.

A mining or lumbering company may develop a town to attract workers and their families. Terrace Bay, on Lake Superior, is a "company town" built by a pulp and paper firm. The company built the houses, recreation center, and stores, and controls the commerce. If the community needs only two barbers, no other barber may move in. Such modern communities are now familiar in northern Ontario.

ONTARIO PLAYS

Canadians have come to terms with their climate. They turn the cold to advantage with winter sports and carnivals. People skate in the open air or under a roof to the sound of music. The frozen surface of the Rideau Canal, which runs through Ottawa, becomes a winter playground stretching for miles. Clerks in downtown Toronto skate at noon or after work on the frozen pool in front of the modernistic City Hall. Girls practice ballet on notched figure skates. Small boys

Ice skating on the rink at the downtown Toronto City Hall has become a favorite lunch hour pastime for many people.

chase a puck on backyard rinks, and playgrounds sprout hockey cushions.

Hockey has become Canada's favorite game, a heritage from the Indians. The first organized hockey game was played on Lake Ontario at Kingston in 1886. Since then, the game has spread across Canada, into the United States, to Scandinavia and Russia. Thousands crowd local arenas, and many more thousands follow all the games on television.

The curling season opens with the coming of winter. Curling is played on iced lanes marked on an indoor rink. Instead of a puck and hockey stick, the players use forty-two-pound granite stones and brooms!

Skiing is very popular, and Ontario provides plenty of hills and usually plenty of snow. Sometimes the snowfall in southern Ontario is light, disappointing the ski resorts. Downhill skiing is the most exciting, but many people have taken up crosscountry skiing. Snowshoeing is having a revival, and webbed tracks lead through many parks. Owners of woodlots prefer them to the noisy snowmobiles.

What the Indians once did for food, today's fishermen do for sport. Hundreds of shacks suddenly appear on frozen lakes. Inside, fishermen angle through holes they cut in the ice, safe from the biting cold. Ice fishing lasts until the returning sun weakens the ice.

With spring, the outdoor sports change and indoor sports such as badminton are forgotten. People are out in their tennis whites, or golf clothes. Boys play catch on the sandlots and baseball in the parks.

The unofficial beginning of summer is Queen Victoria's birthday, celebrated on the Monday before May 24th. Many people use the holiday to "open the cottage," as they spend the Thanksgiving weekend in October closing it. (Thanksgiving in Canada is a general harvest festival, not to be confused with the November holiday celebrated in the United States.)

The cottage is more than a building, it's a way of life in Ontario. The very words call up a picture of sparkling waters, blue skies, and forest crowding a rocky shoreline. It's the time to swim out of doors, to water-ski, to paddle a canoe.

Summer is the time to discover the enchantment of Ontario.

Camping has become a popular summer activity in Ontario. These campers are enjoying the peaceful beauty of a Moose River campsite.

The People
Work in Ontario

Ontario's location makes it a crossroads of transportation. Its wealth in land, forests, minerals, and waterpower lies close at hand.

The job opportunities have drawn people from other countries and other provinces.

A rising population needs more homes and more public buildings. New housing developments must have sewers, electricity, streets, and shopping plazas. The residents need fast roads to get them to work, or subways to cross a big city. Old buildings are torn down to be replaced with taller buildings.

Thunder Bay, at the head of Lake Superior, offers a diversity of work. The two transcontinental railways have large yards there, close to the grain elevators and the ore docks. Its modern cargo terminal welcomes lake freighters and oceangoing vessels. A papermill gives work to men in the bush as well as men in the mill.

All these industries need clerks and stenographers, foremen and sweepers. They need supplies and services from many other companies.

Canada's railroads are very important to the pulp and paper industry.

They support schools and hospitals, stores and restaurants, theaters and sports.

MANUFACTURING

Ontario's industrial growth occurred along with the machine age. New methods were invented, new chemical processes found. Once the pioneering stage was past, growth came swiftly.

Woolen mills replaced spinning wheels, and beer was made in breweries instead of in barns. Grain mills and towering elevators replaced the grist mills beside creeks. Steel mills and foundries made farm tools. An Ontario company won the Grand Award at the Paris Exposition of 1899 for its farm machinery.

A Toronto company manufactured bicycles and in 1901 made a few automobiles. A carriage manufacturer in Oshawa invented the McLaughlin car, and his business grew into General Motors of Canada.

Industry in Ontario surged ahead because of the demands during both World Wars. There was a need for guns and ammunition, trucks and airplanes, as well as for food and clothing.

Most of Ontario's manufacturing is done in the south where most people live. The hundred miles from Oshawa to the Niagara Peninsula is the most industrialized area in the whole country. This was partly the result of cheap power, partly the ports on Lake Ontario.

Factories here make stoves, typewriters, clothing, bricks, cars, and furniture, as well as rubber products, industrial machinery, airplanes, and chemicals. More than half of Canada's printing and publishing is done in the Toronto area.

THE LAND IS RICH

Fifty years ago, most Ontario residents were linked to the land as farmers, fruit growers, grain millers, and dairymen. Today it's the other way around. Five times as many people live in the cities as on the land. Modern machinery replaces the hired help in the fields and farmhouse. Good wages attract people to city professions and factories.

Yet Ontario's farm products lead the country in value. Specialty crops are sold even before the land is plowed. A cannery contracts for acres of peas or tomatoes, or all the cherries of an orchard. Sugar mills even provide seed for fields of sugar beets.

The fertile land of southwestern Ontario produces a wide variety of crops. Apples redden on the slopes of Georgian Bay, and grapes ripen in the "sun parlor" of Niagara Peninsula. Sandy soil produces many tons of tobacco. The black earth of drained marshes raises many thousands of tons of vegetables.

Mixed farms grow wheat for flour and oats for livestock. Dairy cattle graze in green pastures, while beef cattle forage in rougher country. A few farmers raise sheep for meat and wool, and many raise pigs for the famous Ontario bacon. Hardy grains and root crops are grown in pockets of good loam in the Canadian Shield to the north.

Some food factories must be located close to the farms. Companies that can or quick-freeze fruit and vegetables must have them freshly picked. A good labor supply is important to firms that create prepared foods such as cake mixes, pickles, and sauces. Good transportation is vital for the meat packing plants and for mills that turn grain into flour and breakfast foods.

The Ontario government is alarmed that the rather small area of fine farmland is being covered with buildings and highways. "Urban sprawl," the spreading of cities, has gobbled up many farms. Farmers are tempted by very high prices for their land, often more than they can earn by hard work.

WOOD-USING INDUSTRIES

The trees that seemed like enemies to the pioneers soon proved to be a valuable resource. They were exported as masts for the British navy, props for English coal mines, and lumber for building.

Lumber is still important in the construction industry. Hardwood goes into furniture, while spruce and balsam are used in paper. Ontario produces a quarter of Canada's pulp, and its forests provide jobs for a large percentage of Ontario people.

A few years ago, many lumberjacks were farmers who were glad to have winter work for themselves and their horses. Now modern machinery harvests the forest at any time of the year. The men may live in town and go to work in a company bus. Before they start cutting, good roads must be built to carry heavy logging trucks.

Often the logs are hauled by tractor and dumped beside a river. In spring, the river is covered with logs floating down to a sawmill or pulpmill. They are stripped of bark, which is used to fire the boilers. The "waste" resulting when round logs are cut into boards used to be burned. Today that "slash" is shredded and pressed into wallboard.

Logs for a pulpmill pass through immense teeth and are ground into a lumpy, brown porridge. The papermakers add bleach if they want white paper. Then the pulp pours through a series of huge, heated rollers to emerge as paper.

As a population grows, it uses more lumber and more paper. Each summer, students go to the woods and plant tiny trees to replace those that were cut. In this way the forests can keep on growing forever. Unlike minerals, trees are a "renewable" resource.

A MINERAL TREASURE CHEST

Ontario's resources of natural gas and oil are small and limited in area. The crude oil processed in enormous refineries along Sarnia's waterfront is brought by pipeline from Alberta. Underground pipelines distribute oil and natural gas throughout southern Ontario.

The lumber industry makes good use of Canada's rivers. Each spring logs from the logging sites are dumped into a river (left) and floated down to a sawmill or a pulpmill (below).

Apart from petroleum products, Ontario leads the provinces in value of minerals produced. Nickel, copper, iron ore, and zinc enrich Ontario more than its gold and silver. Mines in northern Ontario yield asbestos, lead, gypsum, and a host of other minerals.

Sudbury's treasure was discovered in 1883, when the Canadian Pacific Railway was being laid in the Sudbury Basin. A tie contractor studied a rock cutting, and decided it was copper. He started the first mine.

"But it's not pure copper," the experts said. "It is one-third nickel, that useless stuff that plays the very old Nick in the smelting."

Before long, scientists in the United States and in England learned how to separate the copper from the unwanted nickel. Wealthy men in both countries invested in the copper mines. Then, during the first World War, nickel proved valuable in hardening steel for guns.

The famous Sudbury Basin provides nearly all the nickel outside the Soviet Union. It also supplies more than half the copper, and most of the world's platinum.

Iron ore has been mined north of Sault Ste. Marie for more than seventy years. A vast ore body was discovered west of Thunder Bay in 1949. The mining company had to divert a river and pump out Steep Rock Lake to get at the iron. This was a remarkable engineering feat that took six months.

Mining uses up resources which cannot be replaced, and are finally exhausted. Jobs in the mine and in the industries and services are gone, and the whole community suffers.

The famous gold mines of the Porcupine Lake area began to lay off workers in about 1960. What would happen to Timmins and other towns in the region? Mining men knew the rocks held asbestos, gypsum, rock crystal, and other minerals. An American company quietly discovered rich deposits of base metals—copper, silver, and zinc.

The news leaked out in 1965, and set off an explosion of prospecting. Timmins was saved.

The Enchantment
of Ontario

"The fairest land the heart could wish to see." That's how some early settlers described their new home in Upper Canada.

"Ontario—Keep It Beautiful"is the slogan on automobile license plates. Provincial and civic governments try to live up to the name of their province, "very pretty." Industries landscape their grounds, and most citizens take pride in their gardens.

With its lakes, great and small, its rivers and creeks, its forests and farms, Ontario can rightly claim to be beautiful. Part of its charm is that no city or village is far from fresh water.

THE WATER ROUTES

French and English explorers used the waterways to discover this lovely land. Those ancient routes attract modern boaters, both Canadians and their American visitors. Motorboats and sailboats skim over the waters of the Great Lakes, and canoes dot the lonely rivers of northern Ontario.

Canoeists love the chain of lakes and rivers which forms the boundary between northwestern Ontario and Minnesota. Fur traders paddled their canoes and carried them over the portage trails from Lake Superior to the Lake of the Woods. They noticed the Indian paintings in ocher on the steep cliffs in what is now Quetico Provincial Park.

Temagami and Algonquin, two other provincial parks in the northeast, attract even more vacationers. Each has many summer camps for young people; older campers make long canoe trips into the wilderness.

Almost too many boaters follow the Trent Canal System. It wanders from Lake Ontario through the Kawartha Lakes and Lake Simcoe to Georgian Bay. This waterway was called "The Iroquois Trail," a route familiar to Indians on the warpath.

The rapids and falls have been tamed into "the best-behaved waters in Canada," and the boater does not need to portage even once in 240 miles. Two lift locks and a marine railway carry big boats over the hills.

The Rideau Canal System straggles 125 miles across eastern Ontario from Ottawa to Kingston. Indians followed the Rideau Lake and connecting rivers long ago. Because of the rushing water, they called the Rideau "the singing river."

These falls and rapids are overcome by forty-seven locks and twenty-one miles of canal cut. Barefoot navvies toiled with pick and shovel from 1826 to 1832 to provide a waterway safe from the Americans. Today thousands of Americans and Canadians share its waters in harmony.

The explorers and fur brigades paddled westward up the Ottawa River, down to Lake Huron, through Lake Superior to Thunder Bay. Canoeists today follow in their wake, sometimes covering the whole distance. They respect those *voyageurs* who paddled thousands of miles each year, and carried ninety-pound loads over rough portage trails.

THE PAVEMENT UNROLLS

Most tourists like to discover Ontario by car. They may choose superhighways or quiet back roads. They may choose between friendly roads that link towns and cities, or those that run for hundreds of miles through lonely spruce forests.

The Ontario government sets out picnic tables along most roads, and has established many wayside campsites. Hotels and motels are thick in much-traveled areas, but scarce where the traffic is light.

The explorers' waterway to the west is now flanked by the Trans-Canada Highway. From Montreal it rolls up the Ottawa Valley to Canada's capital.

Ottawa is a beautiful city, unlike the lumbering town of a century ago. The copper-sheathed spires of the Parliament Buildings rise

This lovely roof garden softens the architectural lines of the National Arts Centre in Ottawa.

against a background of Laurentian Mountains in Quebec. Many bridges arch over the Ottawa and Rideau rivers and the Rideau Canal. The handsome City Hall is set on a small island in the river just above the Rideau Falls.

Ottawa's public plantings are highlighted by the Tulip Festival in late May. Queen Juliana and the Netherlands Flower Bulb Institute each donate fifteen thousand tulip bulbs each year. The city buys a quarter of a million more, and citizens plant nearly as many in their gardens. Thirty miles of cycling trails in Ottawa are banked with flowers from early spring to late fall.

Beyond Ottawa, the highway leaves the great bends of the river. It passes through small historic towns such as Arnprior, Renfrew, and Pembroke. It rejoins the waterway at Chalk River, Canada's first atomic power station, and headquarters of Atomic Energy of Canada.

At Mattawa Wild River Provincial Park, the historic and the modern routes bend toward North Bay and Lake Nipissing. The canoe route crosses the lake to descend the scenic French River to Lake Huron.

The Trans-Canada Highway runs north of Lake Nipissing toward Sudbury. Farther west it flanks the North Channel of Lake Huron, a beautiful waterway. The songs of the voyageurs in the winding channel are replaced with the signal toots of freighters.

Some freighters turn back at Sault Ste. Marie, having delivered their cargo of coal or sulphur or limestone. They usually pick up a return cargo of steel rails or ingots of iron ore or pipes or rolls of paper. The city is attractive in spite of its heavy industry.

It is strung out along the bank of St. Marys River, opposite Sault Ste. Marie, Michigan. This is a busy waterway, with five canals on the southern side, one in Ontario. These raise or lower ships about eighteen feet, past the shrunken rapids. A reminder of the fur traders is a segment of a narrow canal built on the Canadian side in 1793 to transport wooden bateaux.

The highway curves northward beside Lake Superior's bold headlands and magnificent beaches. Some campgrounds are filled with tents and trailers every summer night. The scenery is particularly dramatic around Agawa and Nipigon.

At Thunder Bay, the peninsula called the Sleeping Giant overlooks a splendid harbor. In 1970, the twin cities of Fort William and Port Arthur united, and chose the name Thunder Bay. The city is backed by a flat-topped mountain where Thunderbird had his nest, according to Indian legend.

THE TRAIL OF HISTORY

The MacDonald-Cartier Freeway (Highway 401) streaks across southern Ontario from its eastern border to Windsor. Cars and trucks speed over the freeway day and night. Bypassing all settlements, it's a means of "getting there fast."

It parallels an older, more interesting road. Highway 2 threads through historic cities and villages beside the St. Lawrence Seaway. Towns and farmhouses vary from log cabins to Victorian buildings edged with wooden fretwork. Turreted brick and stone houses are reminders of the days of large families and hired help. Old forts which have become National Historic Parks recall a time when Upper Canada had to guard against American invasion.

A series of historical museums include several outdoor folk museums. Pioneer buildings such as schoolhouses and churches have been assembled. The homes are furnished with samples of early industries and crafts.

The largest folk museum is Upper Canada Village near Morrisburg. Through an 1840 tollgate, visitors step back more than a century. Women in pioneer clothing spin, bake bread, hook rugs, and stitch quilts. A stagecoach draws up at the blacksmith shop, and a team of oxen hauls a load of hay. A bateau glides along the little canal, and a rooster crows from the barnyard.

Cornwall, the first Ontario port on the St. Lawrence Seaway, is exactly halfway between the equator and the North Pole. Bridges connect islands to the shores of both Ontario and the state of New York. Dams hold back the waters for use in the canals and in hydro-electric power stations on both banks. The fierce Long Sault Rapids are completely drowned.

The Seaway was planned very carefully to serve the interests of all the people. The federal St. Lawrence Parks Commission reserved thousands of acres for pleasure. Campers and picnickers as well as nature lovers and history hunters enjoy the green spaces.

The old road had to be rerouted when the dammed waters rose above the pavement. Eight villages were wholly or partly flooded, and three new villages came into existence. Over five hundred homes and headstones from fourteen cemeteries were moved. New schools were ready for the students so they didn't miss any lessons.

Ontario's largest cities are strung along Highway 2.

Kingston combines industry with its historic limestone buildings, modern science with Queen's University, founded in 1841. The city stands at the outlet of Lake Ontario, the beginning of the St. Lawrence River with its Thousand Islands. They really total 1,768!

Kingston is the oldest city in Ontario. It was founded in 1673, when Frontenac built his fort to control the Iroquois invaders. It became the center for loyalists who colonized the region, and was briefly a capital. Its shipyards built sailing vessels for the Great Lakes and bateaux for the Rideau Canal.

At one time, Kingston was meant to be "the Gibraltar of the Great Lakes." Fort Henry and a pair of Martello towers were built to guard the southern end of the Rideau Canal. They are now tourist attractions. In summer, schoolboys put on historic British uniforms to go through a precision musketry drill. Occasionally they stage mock battles with a drill squad of the United States Marines.

Highway 2 continues through pretty towns such as Port Hope and Cobourg, and through industrial Oshawa to Toronto.

Old Fort Henry, at the southern end of the Rideau Canal, has become a tourist attraction. In summer, schoolboys don historic British uniforms and stage mock battles.

The capital of Ontario is a city of homes and gardens, of skyscrapers and underground shopping malls. Expressways speed traffic across the city. Subways and one-way streets try to cope with traffic congestion.

Toronto has an unusual form of government. The city itself is only one among six municipalities which form Metro Toronto. Metro spreads over 240 square miles, with a population above two million and still growing. Some attempt is made to contain it with a green belt between the city and the suburbs.

In the heart of Toronto are impressive buildings of mixed architecture. They belong to the provincial government, various hospitals, and the University of Toronto. Close by are the night spots of Yonge Street, the boutiques of Bloor Street, and picturesque Kensington Market. Ontario Place with its concerts, restaurants, and amusements stands by the lakeshore.

The old road west leads into Hamilton, past the blossoming Rock Gardens, the marsh of Coote's Paradise, and restored Dundurn Castle. It curves under the Queen Elizabeth Highway where the Burlington Skyway soars over the bustling harbor.

The "Q.E." skirts the industrial city on its way to Niagara Peninsula, through orchards and vineyards. It crosses the busy Welland Canal. Here lake and ocean shipping bypass the turbulent Niagara River and its 165-foot falls. A scenic parkway runs beside the river from historic Niagara-on-the-Lake to horse-racing Fort Erie.

Highway 2 abandons the lakeshore and strikes inland to Brantford. The city took its name from a ford in the Grand River once owned by Chief Joseph Brant. Here Alexander Graham Bell invented and first used the telephone.

A cluster of three towns a few miles north have merged into one. Galt, Preston, and Hespeler have become Cambridge. Kitchener and

Opposite: Toronto's dramatic skyline. Below: Ontario Place, Toronto's lively lakeside cultural, recreational, and entertainment center.

Many people discover the enchantment of
Ontario by walking over the lovely wooded roads.

Waterloo are physically one, but each keeps its own city government.
Kitchener changed its name during the First World War, when
people rejected the original name of Berlin.

Beyond is London, which its citizens describe proudly as "the
Forest City" because of its tree-shaded streets. The Thames River
winds through the city on its serpentine course to Chatham and Lake
St. Clair. The highway ends at Windsor, the automotive city which
faces *north* to the skyscrapers of Detroit. Many Windsor people use
the tunnel under the river to get to work in Detroit.

Sarnia is located where Lake Huron funnels into the St. Clair
River. The Blue Water Highway curves northward beside Lake
Huron's beaches and resort towns. A spur runs up the length of the
Bruce Peninsula. At Tobermory, it leaps by ferry to lovely Manitoulin
Island, once home of the Great Manitou.

Both the peninsula and the islands are extensions of the Niagara
Escarpment. This limestone ridge runs through western Ontario and
creates the drop at Niagara Falls.

The Martyrs' Shrine in historic Huronia
is near the banks of Georgian Bay.

The 450-mile Bruce Trail runs from Queenston on the Niagara River to Tobermory. The government of Ontario has bought land to preserve the trail for hikers and crosscountry skiers.

Georgian Bay is usually in sight when driving through historic Huronia with its Martyrs' Shrine. A road leading north to Sudbury sweeps past Parry Sound's Thirty Thousand Islands. Another heading for North Bay penetrates the resort country of Muskoka's lakeland.

Beyond North Bay are the towns of Timmins and Kirkland Lake, where gold is still mined. Cobalt's silver mines have become exhausted, but the rocks of the Canadian Shield are still rich in minerals. Cochrane lies in the Clay Belt. To its north, a vast spruce forest cut by long rivers slopes to James and Hudson bays.

Ontario possesses a wealth of natural blessings and a people intelligent in their use and conservation. *"Skanatario,"* murmured the Indians. *"C'est un beau paysage,"* the French declared. We agree, "Ontario *is* beautiful."

Handy Reference Section

INSTANT FACTS

Political:

Became the Province of Upper Canada in 1791; became the Province of Ontario in 1867.

Form of government—Parliamentary

Capital—Toronto

Provincial flower—White trillium

Provincial motto—*Ut incepit fidelis sic permanet* ("Loyal it began, so shall it remain.")

Coat of Arms—St. George's red cross on silver above three gold maple leaves on a green field.

Geographical:

Area—412,582 square miles, of which 68,490 square miles are fresh water.

Largest lake—Nipigon (1,870 square miles)

Longest rivers—Ottawa (696 miles), Severn and Albany (each 610 miles)

Largest island—Manitoulin (1,068 square miles)

Highest point—Tip Top Mountain (2,120 feet)

Lowest point—Sea level

POPULATION

Population—7,703,106 (1971 census)

Population density—18 persons per square mile

Principal Cities	Population	Metropolitan Area Population
Toronto	712,786	2,628,043
Ottawa	302,341	602,510
Hamilton	309,173	498,523
London	223,222	284,469
Winsdor	203,300	258,643

PUBLIC HOLIDAYS

New Year's Day—January 1

Good Friday—Semi-holiday

Victoria Day—Monday before May 24

Dominion Day—July 1

Civic Holiday—First Monday in August

Labor Day—First Monday in September

Thanksgiving Day—Second Monday in October

Remembrance Day—November 11

Christmas Day—December 25

Boxing Day—December 26

ANNUAL EVENTS

Maple Syrup Festival, Elmira—One day early in April
Spring Music Festival, Guelph—First two weeks in May
Folk Arts Festival, St. Catharines—Third week in May
Stratford Festival, Stratford—June to October (drama)
Shaw Festival, Niagara-on-the-Lake—June to September (drama)
Dundurn Castle, Hamilton—July-August (sound and light)
Caravan, Toronto—One week at the end of June (ethnic displays)
Mariposa Folk Festival, Toronto—Early July (folk music)
Highland Games, various locations—July-August
International Sailing Regatta, Kenora—First week in August
Royal Canadian Henley Regatta, St. Catharines—Late July
Rockhound Gemboree, Bancroft—Early August
Canadian National Exhibition, Toronto—Two weeks, ending Labor Day
Oktoberfest, Kitchener-Waterloo—October
Royal Winter Fair, Toronto—Third week in November

PREMIERS OF ONTARIO

John Sandfield Macdonald 1857-71
Edward Blake 1871-72
Sir Oliver Mowat 1872-96
A. S. Hardy 1896-99
George W. Ross 1899-1905
Sir John P. Whitney 1905-14
Sir William Howard Hearst 1914-19
Ernest Charles Drury 1919-23
G. Howard Ferguson 1923-30

George S. Henry 1930-34
Mitchell F. Hepburn 1934-42
Gordon D. Conant 1942-43
H. C. Nixon 1943 (4 months)
George A. Drew 1943-48
Thomas L. Kennedy 1948-49
Leslie M. Frost 1949-61
John P. Robarts 1961-71
William Davis 1971-

YOU HAVE A DATE WITH HISTORY

	Ice Ages
	Indians reach Ontario
1610	Henry Hudson explores coast of Hudson and James bays
1623	Etienne Brule is first white man to see four Great Lakes
1670	Hudson's Bay Company granted Rupert's Land
1673	Fort Frontenac established, now the city of Kingston
1763	Treaty of Paris, by which New France becomes British
1783-	United Empire Loyalists settle Upper Canada
1791	Upper Canada becomes separate province
1793	Importation of slaves prohibited

1812-14	War with the United States, frontier battles
1823-9	First Welland Canal built
1837	The Mackenzie Rebellion
1841	Re-union of Upper Canada with Lower Canada
1848	Fully responsible government begins
1858	Ottawa chosen as capital of the Province of Canada
1866	Fenian raids from the United States
1867	Confederation of four ovinces as Dominion of Canada, July 1
1885	Canadian Pacific Railway completed across northern Ontario
1897	First meeting of the Women's Institutes at Stoney Creek
1917	Women get the vote in Ontario
1959	St. Lawrence Seaway opened
1960	Trans-Canada Highway completed
1967	Air Pollution Control Act passed, result of a radio documentary
1967	First community college of applied arts and technology opened
1968	French-language teacher training established
1969	Ontario Health Services Insurance Plan (OHSIP) established

Index

Italicized page numbers indicate illustrations.